WHAT ABOUT BAPTISM

A WORKBOOK ON WATER BAPTISM FOR KIDS (AND THEIR PARENTS)

WRITTEN & DESIGNED BY
DUANE S. MONTAGUE

©2017 DUANE S. MONTAGUE UPDATED ©2023 DUANE S. MONTAGUE

UNLESS OTHERWISE INDICATED,
ALL SCRIPTURE QUOTATIONS ARE TAKEN FROM THE HOLY BIBLE, NEW LIVING TRANSLATION
COPYRIGHT © 1996, 2004, 2007, 2013, 2015 BY TYNDALE HOUSE FOUNDATION.

USED BY PERMISSION OF TYNDALE HOUSE PUBLISHERS, INC., CAROL STREAM, ILLINOIS 60188. ALL RIGHTS RESERVED.

HEY KIDS!

WHAT IS BAPTISM? WHY DO PEOPLE GET "DUNKED" IN LAKES AND IN WEIRD LITTLE POOLS AT CHURCH? WHY SHOULD I GET BAPTIZED IF I SAY I BELIEVE IN JESUS? AND WHO STARTED THIS IDEA, ANYWAY?

THESE ARE GOOD QUESTIONS.
IF YOU'VE SAID "I WANT TO GET BAPTIZED" TO YOUR MOM OR DAD OR PASTOR RECENTLY, THEY GAVE YOU THIS BOOK TO HELP YOU ANSWER A LOT OF THOSE QUESTIONS AND TO HELP YOU THE BIGGEST QUESTION ABOUT BAPTISM:

AM I READY?

THIS IS A WORKBOOK TO DO WITH YOUR MOM OR DAD OR SOME OTHER "PARENT FIGURE," TOGETHER. IT'S NOT AN ASSIGNMENT FOR YOU TO DO ALONE. IF THEY SAY THAT YOU CAN DO IT ALONE, REMIND THEM TO READ THE NEXT SECTION (FOR THEM). THEY DON'T NEED TO BUG YOU, BUT THEY SHOULD STICK NEARBY AS YOU GO THROUGH IT.

WRITE IN THIS BOOK. YOU CAN MAKE IT MESSY, IF YOU HAVE TO. NO EXTRA POINTS FOR NEAT HANDWRITING. YOU JUST NEED TO MAKE SURE TO ANSWER THE QUESTIONS, READ SOME BIBLE VERSES, AND MOST IMPORTANTLY: BE HONEST. THERE ARE SOME BIG QUESTIONS IN HERE.

ABOUT YOU. ABOUT JESUS. ABOUT YOUR RELATIONSHIP WITH HIM. MOST IMPORTANTLY, I HOPE YOU HAVE FUN AND ENJOY WHAT YOU LEARN!

DUANE

(now give this to your parent to read!)

DEAR PARENTS:

BAPTISM IS A PRETTY COOL MOMENT IN A PERSON'S FAITH, AND IT'S SUPER EXCITING WHEN YOUR CHILD SAYS, "I WANT TO GET BAPTIZED!"

WHETHER OR NOT YOUR CHURCH HAS A "BAPTISM CLASS," YOU PLAY THE MOST IMPORTANT ROLE IN YOUR CHILD'S LIFE AND THIS BOOK WAS CREATED TO HELP YOU HAVE SOME AWESOME AND MEANINGFUL CONVERSATIONS WITH YOUR CHILD. YOU DO NOT NEED TO BE A BIBLE SCHOLAR TO TEACH YOUR CHILDREN SPIRITUAL TRUTHS, AND YOU DON'T NEED TO BE A PASTOR, EITHER. AS A DAD AND A PASTOR, I HELPED CHURCHES CREATE WORKBOOKS LIKE THIS TO MAKE IT AS CLEAR AND EASY AS POSSIBLE FOR ANYONE TO UNDERSTAND THE CONCEPT OF "WATER BAPTISM" AND WHY IT MATTERS. IT'S FOR YOU TO GO THROUGH TOGETHER--WITH THE HOPE IT SUPPORTS YOU AS THE PRIMARY SPIRITUAL LEADER IN YOUR HOME.

PLEASE DO IT SIDE BY SIDE, TOGETHER. IT'S NOT AN ASSIGNMENT FOR YOUR CHILD TO DO ALONE. THE TIME WORKING THROUGH IT TOGETHER SHOULD HELP YOU DETERMINE IF YOUR CHILD UNDERSTANDS THE MEANING OF BAPTISM AND THE VALUE OF THE DECISION THEY MADE TO FOLLOW JESUS.

ONCE YOU'VE COMPLETED THE BOOK, YOU'LL KNOW WHAT TO DO. YOUR CHILD MAY BE READY--YOUR CHILD MAY NEED TO WAIT A BIT LONGER. WHATEVER HAPPENS IT'S OKAY! HOW AWESOME IT IS TO JUST YOUR KIDS GROW IN FAITH!

PRAYING THIS BOOK BLESSES YOU AND YOUR CHILD!

DUANE

FOR PARENTS ONLY:

A FEW TIPS

★ **TAKE YOUR TIME** GOING THROUGH THESE .QUESTIONS.

★ THE VERSES IN THE WORKBOOK ARE FROM THE NEW LIVING TRANSLATION. IF YOU'D LIKE TO USE A DIFFERENT VERSION, **HAVE YOUR BIBLE READY**.

★ **SHARE** YOUR OWN FAITH JOURNEY STORIES WITH YOUR CHILD!

★ CONSIDER **KEEPING A JOURNAL** WITH YOUR CHILD'S ANSWERS TO KEY QUESTIONS (THESE WILL BE A TREASURE WHEN THEY ARE OLDER)!

★ YOU DON'T NEED TO HAVE A BIBLE DEGREE TO KNOW MOST OF THE ANSWERS TO THE QUESTIONS. BUT IF YOU ARE UNSURE, **TALK TO YOUR PASTOR**!

★ THERE IS NO PRESSURE. (SAY THAT AGAIN. AND AGAIN.) KIDS WILL TAKE STEPS IN THEIR FAITH WHEN THEY'RE READY. DON'T TRY TO FORCE ANYTHING!

THE QUESTIONS

Remember to write down what you know! Be honest! (And have fun.)

WHAT IS THE BIBLE? _____
_____

WHAT IS YOUR FAVORITE STORY IN THE BIBLE? _____
_____
_____

WHAT HAPPENED WITH ADAM + EVE? WHAT DID THEY DO?
_____
_____
_____
_____

OKAY, ANSWER THESE:

HAS EVERYONE SINNED?

☑ YES.   ☐ NO.

WHAT ABOUT REALLY NICE PEOPLE?

☑ YES.   ☐ NO.

MORE QUESTIONS

CAN YOU THINK OF ANY SINS YOU'VE DONE?
(don't worry--you don't have to list them out!)

SIN KEEPS US APART FROM GOD. AND SINCE GOD MADE US AND WANTS TO LOVE US, IT MAKES GOD PRETTY SAD.

DID YOU TELL GOD THAT YOU'RE SORRY FOR THE SINS YOU DID?

_____

WHAT DID GOD DO TO RESCUE US AND FORGIVE US FOR OUR SINS?

_____

_____

_____

_____

👍 **HOW DO WE GET FORGIVENESS FROM GOD?**

_____

_____

_____

🎁 **CAN WE JUST BE REALLY GOOD AND MAKE GOD HAPPY? WHY (OR WHY NOT?)**

_____

_____

✝ **WHAT DOES IT MEAN TO BE "SAVED"?**

_____

_____

_____

_____

WHEN WE SING AT CHURCH, IT'S CALLED WORSHIP. WHY DO WE WORSHIP?

_____

_____

LAST QUESTION!

DO YOU HAVE ANY QUESTIONS ABOUT THE BIBLE? WRITE THEM HERE AND SHARE THEM WITH SOMEONE YOU CAN TALK TO ABOUT THEM!

_____
_____
_____
_____
_____
_____
_____
_____

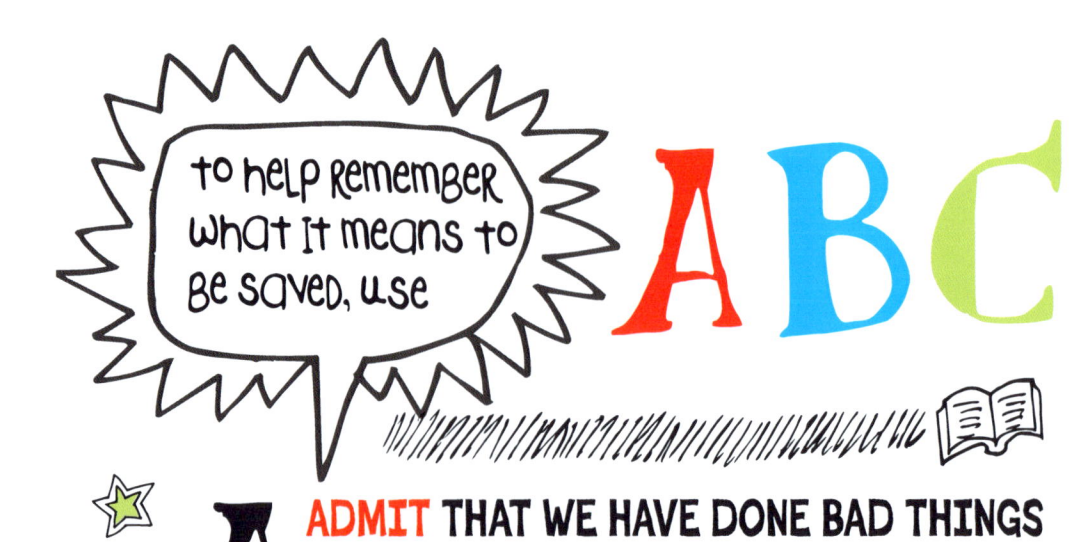

to help remember what it means to be saved, use **ABC**

A **ADMIT** THAT WE HAVE DONE BAD THINGS (THIS IS WHAT SIN IS) AND ASK GOD TO FORGIVE ME FOR DOING THEM.

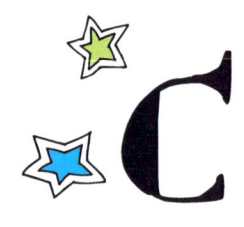

B **BELIEVE** THAT JESUS IS WHO HE SAYS HE IS: THE SON OF GOD! HE'S THE SAVIOR, AND THE ONLY WAY TO HAVE FORGIVENESS FOR OUR SIN AND SEE GOD IN HEAVEN!

C **CALL** ON JESUS AND ASK HIM TO FORGIVE YOU FOR YOUR SINS! ASK HIM TO BE IN CHARGE OF YOUR LIFE AND TELL HIM YOU WANT TO FOLLOW HIM. (THIS IS PRAYER, AND IT'S JUST TALKING WITH GOD--LIKE WHEN YOU TALK WITH YOUR BEST FRIEND.)

yo! THESE ARE JUST SOME **SUPER IMPORTANT**

THINGS TO KNOW

RIGHT FROM THE BIBLE!

God saved you by his grace when you believed. And you can't take credit for this; it is a gift from God. Salvation is not a reward for the good things we have done, so none of us can boast about it! **EPHESIANS 2:8-9**

BEING SAVED FROM OUR SIN IS A GIFT FROM GOD! WE MAKE UNWISE CHOICES AND SIN, WE ONLY NEED TO ASK AND GOD FORGIVES US. WE CAN'T DO ANYTHING TO EARN OUR WAY INTO HEAVEN. IT'S A GIFT FROM GOD BECAUSE HE LOVES US!

what is baptism? what happens?

THE WORD "BAPTISM" MEANS "TO PUT IN THE WATER." BUT BAPTISM IS MORE THAN JUST TAKING A SWIM!

then what is it? tell me, please!

JESUS TELLS US THAT ANYONE WHO BELIEVES IN HIM SHOULD BE BAPTIZED

"And Jesus came and said to them, 'All authority in heaven and on earth has been given to Me. So therefore and make disciples of all nations, baptizing them in the name of the Father and of the Son and of the Holy Spirit, teaching them to observe all that I have commanded you...

MATTHEW 28:18-20

BAPTISM IS A SYMBOL OF THE DEATH & RESURRECTION OF JESUS

Do you not know that all of us who have been baptized into Christ Jesus were baptized into his death? We were buried therefore with him by baptism into death, in order that, just as Christ was raised from the dead by the glory of the Father, we too might walk in newness of life.

ROMANS 6:2-4

IT'S AN OUTWARD SIGN OF AN INWARD COMMITMENT OF FAITH

When they believed Philip as he preached good news about the kingdom of God and the name of Jesus Christ, they were baptized, both men and women. Even Simon himself believed, and after being baptized he continued with Philip... Acts 8:12

IT COMES RIGHT AFTER CONVERSION*

*WHEN YOU DECIDE TO FOLLOW JESUS

those who received his word were baptized, and there were added that day about three thousand souls. Acts 2:41

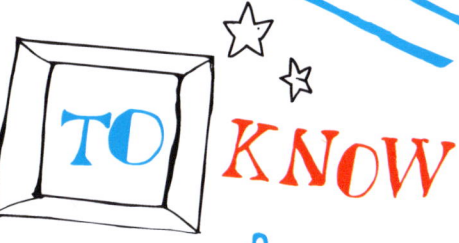

READY FOR MORE THINGS TO KNOW

seriously. are you? because there are a few more things to know, and we can wait until you're ready.

THERE'S A STORY IN ACTS CHAPTER 8 THAT IS VERY COOL! (AND, BONUS! IT EXPLAINS WHAT BAPTISM IS!)

HERE IS AN EXCERPT:
*A LITTLE BIT OF THE STORY FOR YOU

AS THEY RODE ALONG, THEY CAME TO SOME WATER, AND THE EUNUCH SAID, "LOOK! THERE'S SOME WATER! WHY CAN'T I BE BAPTIZED?"

HE ORDERED THE CARRIAGE TO STOP, AND THEY WENT DOWN INTO THE WATER, AND PHILIP BAPTIZED HIM.

Acts 8:36 & 38

TALK ABOUT IT → **HAVE YOU SEEN SOMEONE GET BAPTIZED?** _____

WHAT HAPPENS? _____
_____
_____
_____
_____
_____
_____
_____

But who gets baptized?

Let's look & see

LET'S GO BACK AND READ THE GREAT COMMISSION AGAIN AND DISCOVER EXACTLY WHO IS SUPPOSED TO GET BAPTIZED.

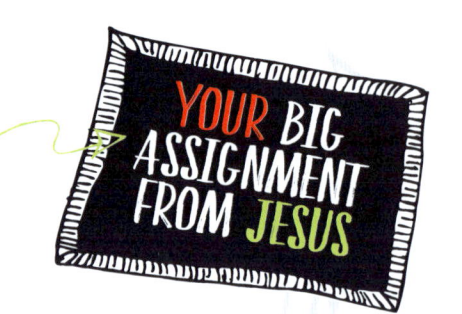

YOUR BIG ASSIGNMENT FROM JESUS

Go therefore and make *disciples* of all nations, baptizing *them* in the name of the Father and of the Son and of the Holy Spirit...

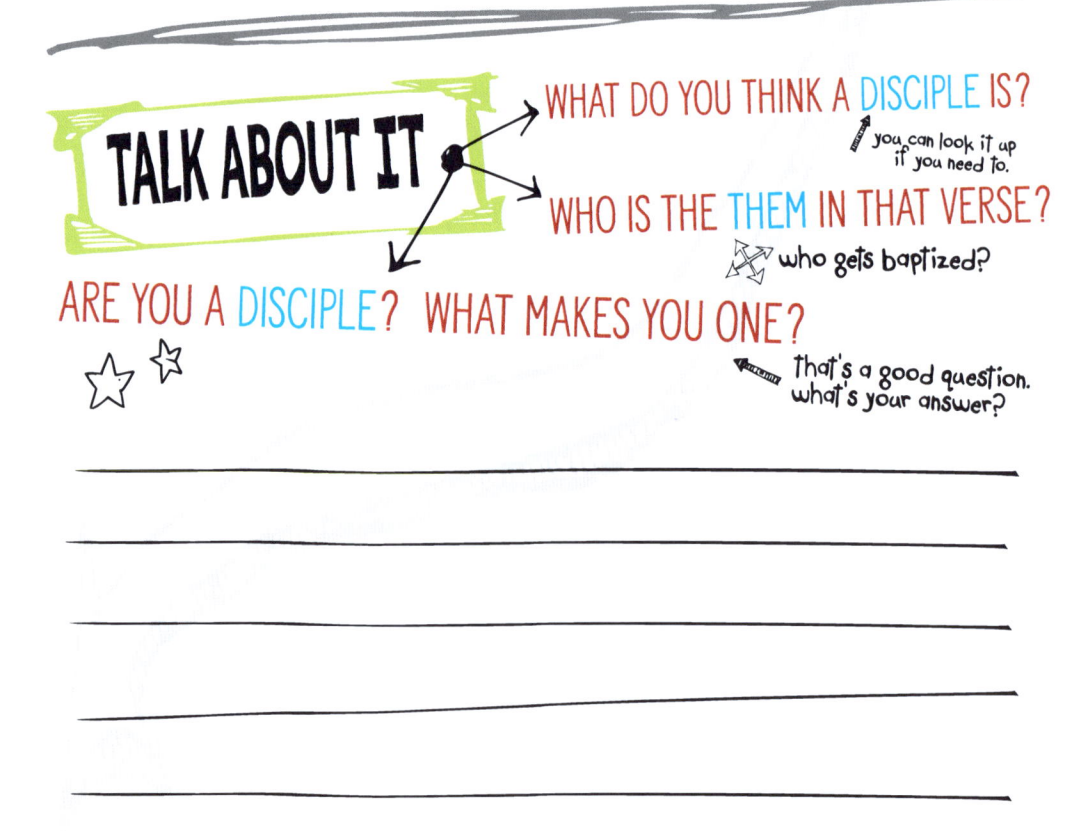

MATTHEW 28:19

TALK ABOUT IT

WHAT DO YOU THINK A DISCIPLE IS?
you can look it up if you need to.

WHO IS THE THEM IN THAT VERSE?
who gets baptized?

ARE YOU A DISCIPLE? WHAT MAKES YOU ONE?
that's a good question. what's your answer?

_____
_____
_____
_____
_____

Why do people get baptized IN water?

WE KNOW THAT **DISCIPLES** ARE THE ONES WHO GET BAPTIZED AND **BAPTIZED** MEANS SOMEONE ELSE DUNKS YOU IN WATER.

BUT WHY?

GET YOUR ANSWER HERE

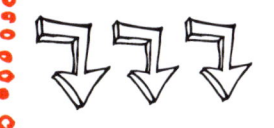

THAT IS WHAT HAPPENED IN BAPTISM. WHEN WE WENT UNDER THE WATER, IT WAS LIKE LEAVING THE OLD COUNTRY OF SIN BEHIND; WHEN WE CAME UP OUT OF THE WATER, IT WAS LIKE ENTERING A NEW COUNTRY CALLED GRACE: A NEW LIFE IN A NEW LAND!

THAT'S WHAT BAPTISM INTO THE LIFE OF JESUS MEANS. WHEN WE ARE LOWERED INTO THE WATER, IT IS LIKE THE BURIAL OF JESUS; WHEN WE ARE RAISED UP OUT OF THE WATER, IT IS LIKE THE RESURRECTION OF JESUS.

ROMANS 6:3-5

WHAT DOES THIS VERSE IN ROMANS MEAN?

WHEN YOU GET BAPTIZED, WHO ARE YOU BEING LIKE?

not sure? read Romas 6:3-5 again!

_____

_____

_____

_____

WHERE DO PEOPLE GET BAPTIZED?

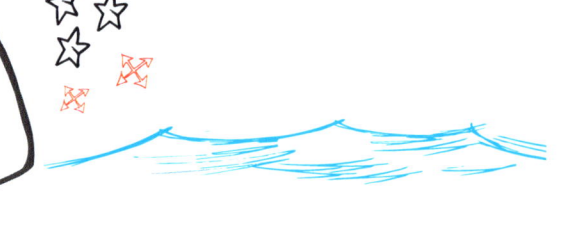

YES, WATER IS KIND OF THE ANSWER. BUT READ THIS VERSE TO GET WHAT WE REALLY MEAN HERE.

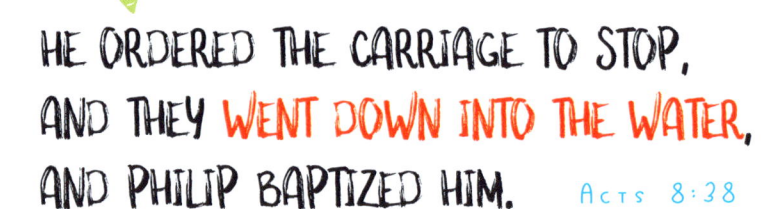

HE ORDERED THE CARRIAGE TO STOP, AND THEY WENT DOWN INTO THE WATER, AND PHILIP BAPTIZED HIM. — Acts 8:38

YOU CAN GET BAPTIZED ANYWHERE, ACCORDING TO THE BIBLE. WHERE DOESN'T MATTER. WHAT MATTERS IS KNOWING WHY YOU GET BAPTIZED--AND THEN DOING IT.

TALK ABOUT IT

DO PEOPLE GET BAPTIZED ALONE (SO NOBODY CAN SEE THEM), OR IN FRONT OF OTHER PEOPLE?

_____

WHY DO YOU THINK BAPTISM IS DONE IN FRONT OF LOTS OF PEOPLE?

_____
_____
_____
_____

SO, WHAT ABOUT BAPTISM? WHY DOES IT MATTER?

write it down right here:

_____
_____

BIBLE VERSES AND STUFF

CAN YOU FIND MORE VERSES ABOUT BAPTISM?

there are 19 in all, so see how many you can find that weren't part of this workbook! there are more than 100 references to baptism in the Bible! (it's kind of a big deal)

_____

_____

_____

_____

_____

_____

_____

WHAT IS YOUR FAVORITE STORY ABOUT BAPTISM?

_____

_____

_____

CONGRATULATIONS!

Guess what? you did it! You read all about baptism! you studied a lot of verses in the Bible, and hopefully you understand just what baptism is now.

7 VERSES!

EPHESIANS 2:8-9
MATTHEW 28:18-20
ROMANS 6:2-4
ACTS 8:12
ACTS 2:41
ACTS 8:36 + 38
ROMANS 6:3-5

write out your favorite!

_____
_____
_____

BUT YOU AREN'T DONE YET. WE STILL HAVE A FEW BIG QUESTIONS

MY TESTIMONY

KIDS -- this part is just for you.

write your answers here on your own.
Let's start with this one.

DO YOU WANT TO GET BAPTIZED?

☐ yes   ☐ no

If you checked yes, keep going!
If you checked no, give this booklet to your parents!

WHY DO YOU WANT TO BE BAPTIZED?

_____
_____
_____
_____

WHAT DOES IT MEAN TO BE A CHRISTIAN?

_____
_____
_____
_____

WHEN DID YOU BECOME A CHRISTIAN?

_____

_____

_____

WHY DID YOU SAY YES TO JESUS?
WHY DID YOU SAY YES TO FOLLOWING HIM AND LOVING HIM?

_____

_____

_____

_____

DO YOU BELIEVE THAT JESUS
HAS SAVED YOU FROM YOUR SIN?   ☐ yes   ☐ no

DO YOU PROMISE TO FOLLOW
JESUS THE REST OF YOUR LIFE?   ☐ yes   ☐ no

KIDS, YOU'RE ALL DONE!
WOW! WAY TO GO!

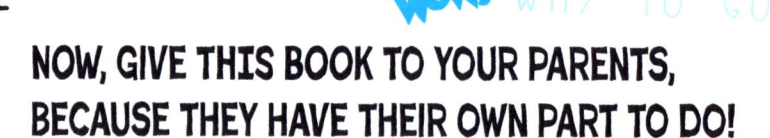

NOW, GIVE THIS BOOK TO YOUR PARENTS, BECAUSE THEY HAVE THEIR OWN PART TO DO!

PARENTS ONLY

PARENTS: NOW COMES THE HARD PART. IT'S VERY TEMPTING TO JUST ASSUME YOUR CHILD IS READY TO BE BAPTIZED. ULTIMATELY, THIS IS AT YOUR DISCRETION. BUT HERE ARE A FEW QUESTIONS TO CONSIDER AFTER REVIEWING YOUR CHILD'S ANSWERS TO THE PREVIOUS QUESTIONS!

- [ ] DOES MY CHILD TRULY UNDERSTAND THEIR SIN?
- [ ] DOES MY CHILD UNDERSTAND JESUS' WORK TO FORGIVE THEM OF THAT SIN AND GIVE THEM A NEW LIFE?
- [ ] HAVE I PRAYERFULLY CONSIDERED MY CHILD'S FAITH? DO I FEEL LIKE BAPTISM IS THEIR NEXT STEP?
- [ ] AM I CONVINCED MY CHILD IS MAKNG THIS DECISION BECAUSE OF THEIR OWN FAITH, AND NOT BECAUSE OF PRESSURE FROM ME OR THE CHURCH?

AUTHOR'S THOUGHTS:

IN MY 20 YEARS OF MINISTRY, WITH MOST OF IT FOCUSED ON HELPING KIDS UNDERSTAND GOD, THE BIBLE, AND THE AMAZING WORK CHRIST DID ON THE CROSS TO BRING NEW LIFE TO ANYONE WHO BELIEVES IN HIM, I HAVE COME TO THE CONCLUSION THAT MOST CHILDREN CANNOT COMPLETELY GRASP THE WEIGHT OF THEIR SIN UNTIL THEY ARE AT LEAST AROUND 7-8 YEARS OLD.

I KNOW THERE ARE SOMETIMES EXCEPTIONS (I HAVE FOUR KIDS WHO HAVE ALL MADE THIS DECISION AT VARIOUS AGES), SO YOU MAY WANT TO TALK WITH YOUR CHILD'S PASTOR OR LEADER.

IT IS ALSO MY EXPERIENCE THAT MANY KIDS WHO ARE BAPTIZED BEFORE AGE 13 WANT TO BE BAPTIZED AGAIN WHEN THEY ARE OLDER, AFTER THEY FEEL THEIR FAITH BECOMES "REAL" AND "THEIR OWN."

WHETHER YOUR CHILD IS READY FOR BAPTISM OR NOT, HERE'S THE **LAST STEP** FOR YOU AND YOUR CHILD TO TAKE.

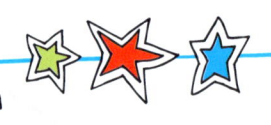

PARENTS:
THANK YOU FOR TAKING TIME TO WALK THROUGH THIS VERY IMPORTANT SUBJECT WITH YOUR CHILD!

IF YOUR CHILD IS READY FOR BAPTISM

REACH OUT TO YOUR CHILDREN'S PASTOR OR LEADER AND ASK FOR DETAILS ON THE NEXT WATER BAPTISM HAPPENING AT YOUR CHURCH. LET THEM KNOW YOUR CHILD HAS COMPLETED THIS WORKBOOK (YOU CAN SHOW IT TO THEM, TOO!) AND CONFIRM YOUR CHILD IS READY! YOUR PASTOR MAY WANT TO CHAT WITH YOUR CHILD TO MAKE SURE THEY UNDERSTAND WHAT BAPTISM IS.

IF YOUR CHILD NEEDS TO WAIT

IT'S OKAY! DON'T FRET.
KEEP PRAYING FOR YOUR CHILD'S FAITH!
CONTINUE FOSTERING YOUR CHILD'S FAITH AND BE READY WHEN YOU AND YOUR CHILD ARE READY TO TAKE THAT AWESOME NEXT STEP!

WHAT HAPPENS NEXT?

WHAT HAPPENS NEXT IS PRETTY IMPORTANT. WHETHER YOU ARE GOING TO GET BAPTIZED OR YOU ARE WAITING, YOU SHOULD **CELEBRATE!**

YOU LEARNED SO MUCH ABOUT A BIG IDEA IN THE BIBLE **AND THAT'S AWESOME!**

THE DAY I WAS BAPTIZED!

ON THE DAY YOU GET BAPTIZED, WRITE DOWN THE DATE IN THIS BOX SO YOU ALWAYS REMEMBER THE BIG STEP IN YOUR FAITH IN JESUS!

thank you for all your hard work! when you get ready to be baptized, remember everything you learned and why it matters. trust god no matter what, because he will always help you make the wise choice as you follow him!

NOTES & STUFF

WRITE DOWN THINGS TO TALK ABOUT LATER

THINGS I'M THINKING ABOUT BAPTISM